Goal Setting

A guide to get you on the track to success

by

Lawrence G Fine

Goal Setting
Copyright © 2009 by (Kick It, LLC)

Table of Contents

Introduction

Goal setting can provide numerous personal and professional advantages; however many of us fail to take advantage of this tool. Without goal setting it can be difficult to attain your desires because it is far too easy to become distracted and sidetracked by outside forces. Goal setting gives you the discipline and control you need to harness your desires and give them force.

Ideally, goal setting should be performed on a consistent routine basis as a way of deciding what it is you want to accomplish and then developing a step by step plan by which these goals can be obtained. Ultimately, the process of goal setting allows you to develop a road map for where you want to go in life. Without the process of goal setting, you are much more likely wander around aimlessly, with no sure direction.

It does require time and concentration to develop goal setting within your own life and you will also need to spend some time updating your goals as old goals are accomplished and new desires form. As you begin to see the difference which goal setting can make in your life; however, the time spent will be well worth the effort.

Understanding why Goal Setting is Important

With sharp, clearly defined goals you gain the ability to measure and take pride in the achievement of what you have accomplished. You take stock of all the hard work which you have put into a process and witnessing the visible results of that work also serves to increase your self-confidence.

Goal setting also gives you the ability to focus your attention and organize your time in order to make the most of your life. This powerful technique provides many more advantages; however.

- Achieve more
- Improve performance
- Increase your motivation to achieve
- Increase your pride and satisfaction in your achievements
- Improve your self-confidence
- Plan to eliminate attitudes that hold you back and

cause unhappiness

Studies have indicated **how** people who use goal-setting effectively:

- suffer less from stress and anxiety
- concentrate better
- show more self-confidence
- perform better
- are happier and more satisfied

The process of goal setting and measurement gives you the ability to see what you have accomplished and as well as what you are capable of achieving. This immediately translates into more confidence and the belief you will be able to achieve goals which might have been even be more difficult.

Goals can be a very important part of the professional workplace. In many cases it is an important part of the appraisal process and strongly effects matters such as raises and promotions.

While goals are quite common in the professional arena,

they also have an important place in other areas of your life. One of the most important benefits of goal setting is it allows you to take control of your life; instead of relinquishing it to others. This control allows you to focus on the things which are personally important to you and define your own level of success.

It is the purpose of this guide to walk you through the steps of creating a goal setting plan as well as to identify and avoid obstacles which could prevent you from achieving your goals.

Before beginning the process of goal setting, it's important to understand a little more about how goals work. If you are interested in setting goals to benefit you in your professional life; it is easy to recognize the fact that your own goal setting can benefit your organization as well. For example; when you achieve the goals which have been laid out for you; it becomes possible for your supervisor to achieve his or her goals which in turn allows the entire organization to achieve numerous other goals.

Many times these goals are expressed as performance

targets, employee satisfaction levels and quotas. The reward for meeting these goals may be extra money on your paycheck, additional time off or a myriad of other benefits.

When companies fail to set goals, both for the organization and the employees; chaos and disaster can ensue. Most companies spend a significant amount of time and money in setting goals in order to ensure their success. There is much we can learn from the business model of goal setting.

One of the most important aspects about personal goal setting which you should understand is, in order for your goal setting to be meaningful, the goals you set should correlate with your personal values. Many people find it helpful to begin the goal setting process by defining their motivations in life through a mission statement. This is similar to a mission statement that most well grounded companies and organizations undertake.

You can begin by writing down words and sentences that you feel describe what you want out of life, the principles which guide you through life and the things you want to achieve out of life.

Like most people, you probably fill more than one role in your life. These may be expressed as wife or husband, grandparent, professional, volunteer, etc. Your mission statement may reflect these roles accordingly.

I am a healthy person who has the wisdom to know what I can and cannot control in my life, and act accordingly.

I work to live and provide for my family. This means financially, emotionally and spiritually.

I am respected in my professional life as being knowledgeable, accessible and eager to learn.

Setting Goals Effectively

The first thing you must understand about goals in order to set them effectively is that they are actually set on different levels. The first step in that process is do decide what you want out of life and to pinpoint the overall goals you would like to achieve. Next, those goals are broken down into smaller goals. These are the targets that you must hit in order to reach the larger, lifetime goals you have set. The final step is to begin working on the plans you have determined are necessary in order to achieve those goals.

In order for your goals to be effective they must meet several guidelines:

Each goal must be positive in nature. Avoid negativity. For example, you might describe your goal as, "Maintain my diet this holiday season." Instead of "Don't overeat this holiday season."

Goals must also be precise. This means they must include a goal, date, time and amount so that they can be easily measured. Such a technique will allow you to gauge when the goal has been achieved. Upon completion of the goal you will have the satisfaction of completing it.

Every goal you set must have a priority. This is especially important when you have set multiple goals. You can avoid feeling overwhelmed when a priority system is in place and will be able to direct your attention to those goals which are most important at the time.

All goals must be written. It is fine to have a goal set in your mind but if it isn't written down it will have very little importance in your life. The action of writing it down gives it the force you need to accomplish it.

If a goal is operational in nature, it should be kept small. This is very important because low-level goals should be small and quite achievable. Otherwise you may feel as though you are making no progress and quickly want to abandon it. Goals that are small and incremental provide more opportunities for reward and give you the drive you need to accomplish larger lifetime goals.

Avoid outcome goals. Instead, set performance goals.

Outcome goal: "I will save some money."

Performance goal: "I will save at least $50 from my next paycheck to put towards a vacation fund."

Always set goals over which you have as much control and power as possible. You can easily become discouraged by failing to meet a goal because of something that was beyond your control. Whether it's bad weather, illness or just a series of unfortunate circumstances; the result will be the same.

Goals should be realistic. In today's pop and media laden culture it can be easy to fall into the goals others have set for you; many of which are quite unrealistic. You must always keep your ambitions and desires uppermost in your mind; not those of others.

At the same time, take the time to understand the nature of your goal well enough so that you do not set unrealistically high goals. This means you must understand the obstacles which could prevent you from achieving your goal as well as the skills which are necessary in order for you to achieve it.

Alternately, goals should not be too low. Otherwise there is not much true satisfaction in achieving them. Goals which are slightly out of your immediate grasp are naturally more attractive and will give you more satisfaction when you achieve them.

Likewise you should not set goals that are unachievable. If you know that you will likely never be able to achieve a goal, there is a strong chance that you won't even put in a little effort to try to do so.

By using goal setting you can decide the things that are important for you to achieve in your life and separate them from those things that are irrelevant. The process of goal setting will also motivate you to achieve those things by building your self-confidence and self-esteem when you look back on the measured achievement of your goals.

When you have achieved your goals, do be sure to take

time to enjoy those achievements. It's also important that you reward yourself appropriately. Enjoy your success!

As with any improvement process, it is also critical that you perform a review of your goal setting and analyze the portions of the process that were successful as well as those that were not. You can use this to improve future performance.

The most successful people in the world are well aware of the fact that the way in which you word your goals has everything to do with their achievement. This includes the wording, structure, format and timing. How you use these elements to frame your goal will strongly effect whether your goals or easy or difficult to achieve. Take a look at the following tips to help you frame your goals in a way in which you will be more likely to achieve success:

Always be specific in the way in which you word your goals. Use precise wording and avoid any phrases that are vague or unclear, such as some, more, etc.

Always quantify measurements. If your goal is to save a

specific amount of money, state your goals as "I want to save $150 this month" not "I want to save some money this month." If you save $2 this month then you have certainly saved some money, but that amount is far different than the specified goal. Stating your goal in this manner helps you to precisely identify your target and know when you have it.

You should also make a point to keep your goals simple in nature. One of the stumbling blocks on the way to creating attainable goals is making them too complex. By keeping your goals clear, simple and focused you will be much more likely to achieve them.

The goals you set must also be something that you care about. If you set a goal that does not matter to you, you won't be very likely to put much effort toward achieving it. If you set a goal that really matters to you; however, you will find that you are anxious to get up in the morning and get started so that you can achieve your goal that much faster.

You will find that in most cases when you set and achieve

a goal it will impact more than just one area of your life. For example, if your goal is to lose 50 pounds you will receive the following benefits: increase your energy and stamina, improve your self-confidence, feel better and lower your risk of developing serious health conditions. The goals that you set must also be measurable.

This is absolutely critical. If you do not take the time to establish a form of measurement for your goals you might as well not even set them at all. Without a form of measurement, how will you know when you have achieved your stated goal? In many ways this ties in directly with stating goals that are specific and clear. For example, stating that you want to be happier is a very vague and ambiguous goal that really cannot be measured.

Instead focus on goals that are specific in nature that you can easily measure in terms of achievement. "I want to obtain a promotion" or "I want to increase my sales by 5% at work" are both examples of clear, specific goals. These goals can both be easily measured and another advantage is that as a result of attaining either of these goals, you may just find that you attain a goal that would otherwise have been unclear and vague; such as achieving more happiness. When defining your goals, focus on terms like dollars, hours, inches, weight, etc.

Always make a point to ensure that your goals are rational. You must define a plan and a path for reaching your goals. If you set a goal that does not make sense and does not have a clear plan for achievement then you are setting yourself up for failure before you even get started.

Goals should be tangible as well. For example, any goal that you set should be something that you can touch, see, hear smell, etc. It should not be something abstract. As previously mentioned, you shouldn't set a goal of becoming happier, but a goal that states "I want to buy a new car this year" will certainly accomplish that, if a new car is what you enjoy.

We mentioned earlier that goals should always be written and this is true for a very good reason. It can be hard to conceptualize something that is not written. You are also much more likely to avoid giving your goal 100% if you have not given it life by writing it down. It can be too easily discarded. The act of writing down your goals, and what is important to you, will help you to cement them in your mind. Don't stop there; however. After you have written down your goals, place them in a prominent location where you can be sure to see them everyday. This will help to keep you focused on what is important to you and on track with achieving your goals.

One of the best ways that you can improve your chances of achieving your goals is by sharing them with those who are close to you. When you have a support team, regardless of your goal, you are more likely to stick with it and do what you need to in order to succeed. While it is important to share your goals with those who are close to you and want you to succeed, it's not a good idea to share them with those people in your life who may not be supportive.

Finally, never set goals that are not in alignment with the values that are important to you. Only you can define those values, but recognize that whatever is important to you must compliment your goals. If the two do not mesh, you will have a conflict on your own and regardless of whether you achieve your goal or not; chances are you will not be happy with the result. So, instead make sure that the goals you set match your values and you will be sure to find success.

Developing a Blueprint for Setting Goals

When first learning to set goals it's important that you develop a template, or blueprint to help you in the process of goal setting. Of course; everyone's goals are different but it is essential that you learn the necessary steps that will allow you to successfully set goals for your future. Such a blueprint can then serve as a sort of checklist for future goal setting.

The first, and also one of the most important steps that you should undertake is developing a desire to achieve the goal you have in mind. In some cases, this step may not even be necessary at all. You may already have an intense desire for the goal you have developed. On the other hand, you may have a goal that you know needs to be accomplished but you do not necessarily have a strong desire for. If you find yourself in this type of situation, one of the ways that you can intensify your desire for the completion of this goal is by taking the time to sit down and write out all the benefits and advantages of the completed goal.

So, how many advantages and benefits should your list contain? The number may be unique for each individual, but at a minimum it should contain 50 benefits and preferably more than that. In the beginning, it may seem as though it would be difficult to come up with that many benefits, especially about a goal that you do not already have an intense desire to accomplish, but you will be surprised at how quickly the list will come together once you start working on it. Rather like a snowball, it will gain momentum as it grows. In addition, as you see the list of advantages and benefits grow, your desire to accomplish the goal will likewise expand.

When developing a desire for your goal, it is also important to make sure that the goal you set does not contradict with your values. In an earlier section, we mentioned the importance of determining your values during the goal setting process. This is because this is an extremely important element of goal setting. Any goal that you set should never conflict with any other goal that you have set for yourself.

The next step will be to write down your goal. As we have

already established, the act of writing down your goal is extremely important; this is what makes it takes life and become substantial.

Remember when writing down your goal, to be as specific as possible. It's not enough to simply say that you want to save some money, make more money or purchase a new car or home. This is very broad thinking and will not necessarily help you to gain the goal of your dreams. For example, there is a tremendous difference between saying that you want to purchase a new home and stating that you want to purchase a new home with 3000 square feet and an in-ground swimming pool.

Always be as specific as possible when you write down your goal and you will be able to overcome the temptation to settle for less than your dreams.

While it can be extremely tempting to skip straight from writing you're your goal to working on the steps necessary to obtain it, you are setting yourself up for almost certain failure if you do not take the time to identify possible obstacles that you will need to overcome in order to accomplish your goal. Along this same regard, you also need to identify the sources that will be necessary to help you overcome these obstacles. These sources may include knowledge, organizations or people. Whatever obstacles you feel you may run into during your efforts to accomplish your goal should be written down clearly along with sources you need to overcome them.

Many people feel they work best under pressure and with a deadline looming. With that in mind, it's always imperative that you set a deadline for your goal. This will help you to analyze where you are now in relation to the achievement of your goal and then measure how long you believe it will reasonably take you to complete the goal.

Remember when setting a deadline for your goal that reason is a key factor. You will achieve nothing you set a deadline that is completely unreasonable and you are quite naturally unable to achieve your goal by that deadline. Instead, it's much better to set a deadline that is quite reasonable and one that you believe you can naturally live with. Also remember to add in time for overcoming obstacles as well as delays.

The next step in developing a blueprint for setting your goals is to develop a plan. This means you need to list all activities related to the achievement of your goal and then prioritize them. Once you have the list prioritized, rewrite it in priority order and make any corrections that are needed.

At this point you need to gain a clear mental picture of the goal. Do not view it as you see it now, but try to gain a clear picture of the goal as it would be accomplished. If your goal is to save a certain amount of money to make a down payment on a home or a new car, then imagine yourself actually purchasing the home or car or whatever. Take the time to savor how that moment will feel. The picture and emotions that picture evoke will be one of the tools you use to help you through the act of actually accomplishing your goal as well as overcoming obstacles along the way. When it feels as though you are not making progress or feel as though you want to give up, you will need to replay that picture in your mind.

One technique that many people find to be quite helpful in

visualizing their goals is to create a storyboard for their goals. This can be accomplished quite simply by purchasing an inexpensive piece of poster board and attaching photos related to your goal to the poster board. You can obtain suitable photos from a variety of sources, if you don't already have an actual picture. For example, consider magazines and brochures. You can put as many pictures as you like on your collage and watch it grow as you accomplish the tasks necessary to obtain your goal. As you view the collage everyday, you will be more likely to stay on track with the plans and tasks necessary to achieve that goal.

The final step in developing a blueprint for the accomplishment of your goals is to impart it with persistence, resolve and determination. Remember that you should never give up, even when you run into obstacles. Instead play the mental picture you have developed in your mind of how it will feel when you accomplish your goal and allow that to carry you through difficult periods.

Now that you have a blueprint for setting goals, it's time

to look at the areas in your life where you can set goals. There are basically six areas of life where goals can be set. They are:

- Family and Home
- Spiritual and Ethical
- Social and Cultural
- Financial and Career
- Physical and Health
- Mental and Educational

Many people tend to focus on one area of their life when setting goals, such as financial and career and virtually neglect the other areas of their life. This is very dangerous thinking. One of the biggest problems with this type of strategies is that it does not allow you to ensure a balanced life. Sure, you may end up accomplishing all of your financial goals but you may do so at the expense of your health, family, home and ethics.

Financial and Career
Do you enjoy your work? Do you feel you are making a contribution to society? Are you living up to your poten-

tial? Have you achieved a satisfactory standard of living? Have you planned for your children's education? What about your own retirement?

Social and Cultural

Does your circle of friends enrich your life and contribute to your sense of fulfillment and well-being? Is there at least one other person with whom you can discuss important life experiences? Do you have interests outside of your career and family (e.g., sports, theater, outdoor events)?

Spiritual and Ethical

Have you ever articulated specific personal values to yourself? Are you living up to those personal values? Is religion important to you? If so, are you happy with the way you are practicing your religion? If not, have you reconciled your relationship with a higher power or with the universe in general?

Family and Home

Have you realized your dream in terms of your home and family relationships? Be sure to use your own personal standards rather than society's standards.

Mental and Educational

Did you accomplish the educational goals you set for yourself following high-school graduation? Are you still growing and learning? Do you invest in your continuing education on a regular basis?

Physical and Health

How satisfied are you with your current level of physical health? Are you living up to your own standards in terms of diet and exercise? Are you fit enough to do the things you want to do?

Remember that when you practice setting goals that are inside your values you will never set a goal that is direct contradiction with any of your other goals. By taking the time to ensure that you have goals set in the six major areas of your life, you will be able to ensure that you not only have a balanced life but that you do not contradict your values system either.

For some people, it can be difficult to look far into the future to determine what goals you want to accomplish five, ten, fifteen or more years from the present time. If you find yourself falling into that category, one way that you can help yourself out of this trap is by defining the things that you want most this year. Start by making a list of the ten things you want most.

When making the list, you should remember to focus on the six main areas of your life. If you do that, you can easily find that you have six goals you would like to accomplish this year. More than likely, as you work on completing your list you will find that you have difficulty in limiting your list to just ten goals for this year.

Goals I want to Accomplish this Year 20_____
Family and Home
Spiritual and Ethical
Social and Cultural
Financial and Career
Physical and Health

Mental and Educational
Goal #7:
Goal #8
Goal #9
Goal #10

A technique that you can use to begin establishing more long term goals is to think of the three most important things you want to accomplish before you die.

Take a look at this template to help you get started.

Goal
#1:_____
Obstacles:_____

_____

_____

Resources to overcome obstacles:

_____

_____

_____

Steps to Achieve goal:

_____

_____

Goal

#2:_____

Obstacles:_____

_____

_____

Resources to overcome obstacles:

_____

_____

_____

Steps to Achieve goal:

_____

_____

Goal
#3:_____

Obstacles:_____

_____

_____

Resources to overcome obstacles:

_____

_____

_____

Steps to Achieve goal:

_____

_____

After you have established goals for the 10 most important things you want to accomplish this year and the 3 most important things you want to accomplish before you die you can then begin working on lists of things that you want to accomplish within the next twenty years, ten years, five years and finally to the three most important things you want to accomplish within one day.

Motivation And Goal Setting Worksheet

1. What are your life time goals?

    _____

    _____

    _____

    _____

    _____

2. What are your goals for the next three to five years?

    _____

    _____

    _____

    _____

3. What are your goals for this coming year?

_____

_____

_____

_____

_____

4. What are the things you need to do in order to accomplish this year's goals?

_____

_____

_____

_____

_____

In some cases, you may find that the goals you set on a short term basis are actually activities that will allow you to accomplish more long term goals. For example, saving a certain amount of money this month or year may allow you to save for the down payment you need to purchase a new home or car; which is a more long term goal.

When setting these goals it's important to establish the difference between wishing for things and actually setting a plan in action that will allow you to accomplish them. This is the major difference between dreaming and goal setting.

In order to ensure that you are actually doing something that will allow you to achieve your dreams it's important to ask yourself good questions related to how and what you can do to make your dreams a reality.

For every goal that you set, be sure to ask yourself the following questions:

What are the circumstances within which this goal will be realized?

Who

What

_____

When

_____

Where

_____

Why

_____

You also need to focus on the outcome of your goal in order to solidify it in your mind. Take a look at the following questions that can help you in this regard.

Q. What good will happen if you get the outcome?

A._____

Q. What good will happen if you don't get the outcome?

A._____

Q. What won't happen if you are successful?

A._____

Q. What won't happen if you are unsuccessful?

A._____

Q. Is there a reason that you might be hesitant to obtain the goal?

A._____

Q. Is there any reason to believe that this idea will not work?

A._____

While it is important that you have multiple goals set in order to focus on the six major areas of your life, it is also equally important that you only focus on one project at a time. At first this may seem to be a contradictory statement; however one of the biggest mistakes that many people make in goal setting is in trying to work on too many things at once. What generally results is chaos.

This is where making a to-do list or goals for the day list can become extremely helpful. This type of list will help you to focus on the tasks that are important in order to accomplish the most pressing goals. While it may be more enjoyable to work on your goal of improving your golf game, this goal may not be as pressing or imperative as working on your goal to increase your sales so that you can achieve the promotion and raise you need in order to achieve your goal of purchasing a new home within the next year.

When you have several goals set at once, taking the time to prioritize the activities related to the achievement of those goals is absolutely critical. Without such steps, you will find it increasingly difficult to focus on the most important tasks without becoming delayed and side tracked by other activities.

The first step in prioritizing your goals is to actually sit down and rank them according to importance. For example, after you have set goals for the 10 most important things you want to accomplish this year, it will then be necessary to rank them according to importance.

When ranking your goals, consider factors such as which goals will contribute the most growth for you professionally/personally?

You might consider adding a priority ranking of A, B or C to your list of goals. According to this priority system:

A: Goals that have the highest value and immediate concern

B: Goals that have medium value and secondary importance

C: Goals that have least value and importance

Chances are that when you have completed the ranking of your goals you will find that you have multiple priorities A goals. In this case you will then need to separate them and rank them according to importance.

#1 PRIORITY: _____

(Time needed to complete_____)

Goals:

(_____) _____(___/___/___)

(_____) _____ (___ / ___ / ___)
(_____) _____ (___ / ___ / ___)
(_____) _____ (___ / ___ / ___)
(_____) _____ (___ / ___ / ___)

#2 PRIORITY: _____

(Time needed to complete_____)

Goals:

(_____) _____ (___ / ___ / ___)
(_____) _____ (___ / ___ / ___)
(_____) _____ (___ / ___ / ___)
(_____) _____ (___ / ___ / ___)
(_____) _____ (___ / ___ / ___)

#3 PRIORITY: _____

(Time needed to complete_____)

Goals:

(_____) _____ (___ / ___ / ___)
(_____) _____ (___ / ___ / ___)
(_____) _____ (___ / ___ / ___)
(_____) _____ (___ / ___ / ___)
(_____) _____ (___ / ___ / ___)

#4 PRIORITY: _____

(Time needed to complete_____)

Goals:

(_____) _____ (___/___/___)

(_____) _____ (___/___/___)

(_____) _____ (___/___/___)

(_____) _____ (___/___/___)

(_____) _____ (___/___/___)

#5 PRIORITY: _____

(Time needed to complete_____)

Goals:

(_____) _____ (___/___/___)

(_____) _____ (___/___/___)

(_____) _____ (___/___/___)

(_____) _____ (___/___/___)

(_____) _____ (___/___/___)

After you have written a detailed plan for each goal, including the following:

• Specific details

- The unit of measurement you will use to assessment the achievement of your goal

- How your goal will be achieved

- Obstacles you will face in achieving your goal and resources you can use to overcome those obstacles

- Timeframe for achieving your goal

You will then need to identify the steps that will be necessary for you to accomplish your priority A goals. These activities should then be listed in sequential order. Determine how much time you will need to accomplish each of these activities and then set a separate time frame for each activity. Because of the fact that a deadline is simply not enough for many people to get on track and stay on track, it's also a good idea to establish and exact start and finish date. This will help to ensure that you are not late in getting started on the steps necessary to complete your goal and therefore do not give into unrealistic timeframe expectations.

Task:	Target Date:	Date Completed:

Don't forget to include milestones along the way to help you measure your success and ensure that you are on the right track. When setting milestones its important to also include information that can help you to determine what you expect to achieve by each milestone. Consider this as a sort of goal setting check-up.

Now that you have your overall goals set as well as your goals prioritized and a list of activities that are necessary in order for you to complete those goals, it's time to develop a daily and weekly schedule. You can do this by reviewing the list of activities you have drafted and the corresponding timeframes.

Many people find that it helps them to check off activities as they complete them on the path to achieving their goals. This can provide you with a sense of definite accomplishment and prevent you from feeling as though you are not doing enough to accomplish your goals, especially long term goals. For example, if one of your long term goals is to obtain a college degree it can be quite easy to feel as though you are drowning in a myriad of small details throughout the years of college work that are necessary to achieve your ultimate goal.

By performing several check-ups on the milestones of your goal and checking off major activities as they occur (finishing first semester, beginning work on thesis, etc.) you can begin to see that you are gradually whittling away at the steps necessary to obtain your overall goal.

When you are performing check-ups for your goal it's also important to perform evaluations to determine whether your goals are still realistic and obtainable. You may find it is necessary to make some adjustments in order to compensate for other factors. Perhaps something has occurred that makes the attainment of a goal previously not as important more critical. In some cases you may find you need to adjust your timeline in order to compensate for events outside your control and caused delays.

Weekly Plan

Date:

Activities Required to Accomplish Objectives	Priority	Time Needed	Day

Forming Goal Statements

Now that you have a clear idea of how goals are set it's time to actually get down to the business of setting your goals and the first step in the process is forming a goal statement. The importance of this step cannot be overlooked because it sets the basis for the entire process. In other words, the success and failure of your goal depends on how you form your goal statement, so it's important to formulate a clear and accurate goal statement.

While this may seem to be a daunting task at first, it becomes quite easy when you follow a simple plan. This plan is referred to by many life coaches as the SMART acronym. SMART stands for:

Specific

Measurable

Action-Oriented

Realistic

Time and Resource Constrained

First, all goals you set should be specific enough so you always know exactly what it is you are working toward. Your goals should also be measurable so you are able to determine when your goal has been achieved. In terms of action, your goal should have activities attached to it that will produce results and finally your goal should be timely with a definitive timeline for completion.

Let's take a look at a few examples of goal statements to begin seeing how statements can either fit this profile or fall outside of it.

"Purchase a new home."
"Purchase a 3000 square foot home with an in-ground swimming pool within two years."

"I want to make a lot of money."
"I want to increase my annual income to $75,000 within the next five years."

"I want to own a Mercedes Benz."
"I want to purchase a pre-owned Mercedes Benz within the next two years."

"I want to save money for my retirement."

"I want to save $500,000 for my retirement by age 65."

"I want a promotion."

"I want to achieve a promotion to vice-president of marketing affairs within three years."

As you can see there is a huge difference between forming a goal statement that is vague and forming a goal statement that is specific, measurable, action oriented and time constrained.

Rather than use the SMART acronym, some people find it more beneficial to pose a series of questions to each of their goal statements. Questions that can help you evaluate the effectiveness of your goal statement include:

What will be different when I achieve this goal? If after posing this question to your goal statement, you cannot determine that anything in your life will be different then you need to go back to the drawing board and revise your goal statement.

How will I know I have achieved this goal when I see it?
You must be able to determine when your goal has been accomplished. In the example listed above, the goal of saving money for retirement is far too broad and vague. There is a significant difference between saving $5 and $500,000 for retirement, but yet with this type of goal statement both scenarios meet the specifics of the statement in its original form.

What is the optimum performance level of this goal? If you do not take care to set a performance level for your goal, there may be a strong temptation to not perform as well as you can to achieve it.

What constraints, if any, might affect the performance of this goal? As always, it's important to define any obstacles you may encounter when setting your goals so you know what you need to overcome in order to achieve it.

When defining your goal statements, it's also important to take a look at the exact terminology you use. Avoid using words that are clearly vague in nature such as the following:

Appreciate   Recognize

Attitude   Hear

Familiar with   Interest in

Feelings for   Knowledge of

Capable of   Listen to

Conscious of   Adjust to

Confidence in   Responsive to

Experience   Think

Attitude   Understand

Realize

Consider the following goal statement template:

"I commit to having _____ on or before

_____ by doing _____ and because

_____."

The Connection between Dreams and Goals

When beginning to set your goals it's important to understand both the connection between dreams and goals as well as the significant differences. Most people have dreams and daydreaming is a favored hobby among a large portion of the world. However, there are important factors that make the difference between those individuals who achieve their dreams and those who continue to go about their daydreaming without ever realizing the attainment of their dreams.

That difference is goal setting and it turns an aimless dream into a driven goal.

In order to move a dream from hazy landscape of daydreaming into reality, you must give it a vehicle in which to move and the fuel of activities and tasks.

Without providing these important elements, your dream is very likely be left up to chance and luck. You can significantly increase the odds of achieving your dream, no matter how unattainable it may seem at the time to you, by clarifying it, providing specific details, defining it so you can see it, feel it and know it when you see it.

Even if you feel a dream is too difficult to achieve, you can improve your chances by defining it as a goal. This makes it concrete and helps to assure that opportunities will not go by unnoticed. The process of goal setting also gives you a step by step plan so that you know exactly what you need to do in order to achieve your dream and helps you to avoid detours and dead ends that might distract and delay you on the way to achieving that dream.

The Makeup of Good Goals

Realizing the difference between good goals and goals that are simply time wasters is imperative. A good goal is a goal that is written, challenging, believable, specific, measurable and contains a specific deadline.

When writing your goals, realize you have numerous options available to you. The most traditional method is the pen and paper method and this works quite well for many people. For other people; however, the act of writing down goals on a sheet of paper is not very efficient. The paper is too easy to misplace or even completely lose. If it helps you, use a word processing program or any other software you find helpful for writing down your goals. The important point here is they be written down. They do not specifically need to be written on paper.

In terms of believability the goal must at least be believable by you. This does not necessarily mean others must believe your goal. In fact, in many cases you may find there are numerous people who will not believe you can accomplish your goal. This does not make the goal any less achievable or worthy. It simply may mean you need to work a little harder at achieving it.

It is important when setting your goals to set some goals that are challenging. All of your goals should not be so simple that you do not need to stretch yourself in order to achieve them. There is very little satisfaction or accomplishment in achieving goals of this nature. That said; however, not all of your goals need to be challenging. One of the steps necessary in order to complete a larger long term goal may involve a smaller goal that is not nearly as challenging as the big goal.

One of the great things about easy goals is they build a sense of follow-through, responsibility and reward. They also allow you to feel the joy of gratification for your efforts.

While not all goals must be challenging, all goals should be measurable and specific. This means they should not be vague or ambiguous so you do not know when they have been completed.

One of the new trends in goal setting may dictate that goals no longer need a deadline; however, it still remains true most people work better when there is a specific deadline in place. This allows you to know exactly how much time you have remaining in which to complete your goal and perform periodic check-ups along the way to make sure you are on the right track.

There is a fine line between establishing goals that are challenging and realistic. Ideally, a goal should be both but it can admittedly be difficult to determine when a goal fits both of these criteria. Generally, a goal is realistic if you have enough time and effort to accomplish it. Keep in mind the goals you accomplish should depend on what you have the most control over, not factors that are controlled largely by others. For example, winning the lottery is a goal is based on a random event and while there may be some minor things you could do to improve your chances of winning the lottery; the results would still be largely dependent on random events.

If the majority of the goals you set are not realistic, you run the very real risk of becoming frustrated and disappointed when you are not able to accomplish a large portion of your goals. This does not mean you should not attempt goals that seem very challenging or that defy what appear to be the odds. Some of the most successful people in the world have done just that and obtained the goals they sought. Just make sure you have a nice balance.

All goals should be broken down into smaller, more manageable goals that can be worked on individually. This will prevent you from becoming overwhelmed. These smaller goals are often referred to as baby steps and they are a great way to build confidence and a solid track record.

Tips for Avoiding Obstacles in Goal Setting

There are several areas in the goal setting process you need to watch out for in order to avoid obstacles. Let's take a look at a few.

It is important you remain focused on the goals you have set for yourself and one way to do this is by avoiding the temptation to set too many goals at one time or are scheduled to become due at the same time. While there is nothing wrong with having a large number of goals going at the same time, you can quickly run into trouble if you have several of those goals are due at approximately the same time. Be realistic in the amount of time you can dedicate to each goal.

At the same time it's important not to limit yourself by only assigning simple and easy goals. Always make it a point to be working on one simple goal and one difficult goal at any given time. As these goals are accomplished, you will become motivated by your own success, which will then spur you on to accomplishing other goals. Along the same lines, make it a point to be working on at least one short term goal and one long term goal. The short term goals are usually simpler in nature and will give you the confidence you need to accomplish more difficult goals as you realize frequent victories. Long term goals are those that generally will require two years or longer in order to complete. Goals that require less time than this to complete can be categorized as a short term or mid-range goal.

When setting your goals make sure you are setting performance goals and not outcome goals. Outcome goals can quickly lead to disappointment because the goal is focused on the end result and not the performance. This type of goal is too easily affected and influenced by reasons out of your control.

Always be realistic in the goals you set. The general rule of thumb is if you cannot even believe in your goal then there is virtually almost no chance you will be able to achieve it.

At the same time, do not give in to the temptation to set goals so low there is really no sense of accomplishment, or benefit in achieving them. In this case, you are wasting valuable time. Always work on goals that are challenging to you.

The importance of setting goals that are specific and clear cannot be stated enough. It can be difficult to know when you have achieved goals that are vague because these types of goals can be difficult to measure.

As previously discussed, it is extremely important you prioritize not only your goals but the action steps required to accomplish your goals. Realize; however, when you are prioritizing your goals you need to be flexible in doing so. When necessary, change due dates or put a goal on hold if you need to make changes.

As you work with goal setting you will probably notice after awhile it is possible to combine certain goals and tasks. Whenever possible, it's a good idea to do this. This is simply good time management and it will allow you to achieve even more in less time.

Finally, make it a point to be balanced in all you do. Work

on setting goals in the six major areas of your life and always be sure your goals do not conflict with your own values.

FAQ about Goal Setting

How many goals should I have at the same time?

This is really a personal decision. A large number of goals is considered to be anything in excess of 7 goals set at one time. You, and you alone, will need to determine how many goals you can realistically set at one time without spreading yourself too thin.

The number of goals you can reasonably set at one time very well may vary and change as phases of your life change. You will quite likely be able to set and dedicate time to more goals when you do not also have the added responsibility of raising young children, for example.

While it is important not to set so many goals at one time that you become overwhelmed, do be sure not challenge yourself with the goals you have set. Remember it is possible to set goals that do not begin until a future date even while you are focusing on current events in your life.

How many goals can I "work on" at the same time?

Once again this depends entirely on you as an individual and also what you believe "working on" to mean. For example, you may have a goal set you would like to accomplish by next year but it's not necessary to begin working on the activities for that goal at the current time. In this case, the goal is set but you may not necessarily be working on it.

Don't allow this theory to cause you to set so many goals you become overwhelmed; however. Always remember you only have a certain number of hours in the day and there are certain tasks and responsibilities that must be addressed regardless of the number of goals you have set. It is far preferable to set a lesser number of goals and achieve more of them than set an unrealistic number of goals and achieve none of them.

For most people, a manageable number of goals ranges between five and ten. This of course, depends on several factors:

How focused can you be to working on your goals?

For example, if you know there is a lot going on right now in your life, it's not a good idea to set a large number of goals. Instead focus on a small number of goals that are important to you.

How difficult are your goals?
Only you can decide the complexity level of your goals, but do realize you should have a mix of some challenging and some easy goals.

Are your goals short-term or long-term?
If you have a mix of short term and long term goals as recommended then you will be able to avoid having too many tasks coming due at the same time. If; however, you set a large number of short term goals then you may very well become overwhelmed by the tasks that are facing you and you will find you need to have less goals set.

What if my goals conflict with each other?
While it is true almost all of your goals will require some of your resources such as time, money, effort, attention, etc. it is important that your goals are not ultimately at odds with one another. They should not conflict with your

intrinsic values. If you find your goals are constantly at odds with one another you need to sit down and do some serious revisions.

The Ten Basic Rules of Goal Setting

Rule # 1: Be Decisive in your goal setting.

The responsibility for making all decisions relating to your goals ultimately resides with you. Recognize this early on take the actions you need to in order to decide what you want, why you want it and what needs to be done in order to obtain it.

Rule # 2: Stay focused

It can be very easy to get sidetracked in the process of obtaining your goals, especially when dealing with long term goals; however it will always be your ability to maintain a strong focus will be a determining factor in whether you are able to achieve your goals or not.

Rule #3: Be Open to Failure

It's quite one thing to be confident in your abilities and another to be able to accept the fact that failure is sometimes a part of life and be able to learn from it. It is only from being able to accept that failure sometimes occurs and being able to evaluate it objectively and learn from it that you will be able to go on to future successes.

Rule #4: Always Write Down your Goals

When a goal is not written down it is far too easy to push it to the far recesses of your mind when your life becomes burdened with other pressing needs. Take the opportunity to create success for yourself by writing down your goals and committing them to an action plan.

Rule #5: Plan for your goals

No goals can be accomplished without planning, unless sheer luck intercedes. Without proper planning, you can always expect you will fail more times than you will succeed.

Rule # 6: Get others involved

One of the best things about achieving a goal, regardless of what it happens to be, is in enjoying and sharing the success of that moment with others. When you allow others to become involved in your goals you not only provide another source of wisdom and knowledge you can tap into to overcome potential obstacles, but you give yourself your own personal cheering section.

Rule # 7: Take action

Goals cannot be achieved without action oriented steps. You must divide your goals up into tasks you can accomplish in manageable sections or you can expect your goals will always remain distant dreams.

Rule #8: Reward yourself

History has shown throughout time that people just naturally respond better when there is an incentive at state. Think of things that will give you pleasure when you accomplish even small goals can help you to achieve larger goals. Take the time to enjoy your success and reward yourself for your persistence, dedication and hard work.

Rule # 9: Don't forget to inspect your goals

Performing inspections along the way is the best way to
maintain a healthy goal system. This allows you to be
proactive and discover any small problems with your goal
plans before they become major obstacles.

Rule #10: Always maintain your personal integrity
This rule cannot be stressed enough because it is
extremely important. It is imperative you maintain your
personal integrity and never set goals that will conflict
with your own personal values.

Exercises in Goal Setting

Exercise 1: Writing a goal statement

Write a brief summary statement of a goal you would like to accomplish. Be sure to include such factors and details as cost, timing, location, etc. Be as specific as possible.

Goal Statement:_____

_____

_____

Exercise 2: Measure of success and goal assessment

Remember the measure of success is how you will know when you have achieved your goal and to what degree your goal has been achieved.

Write specific, measurable statements as to possible outcomes. Whenever possible give yourself a range of results that will allow you to stay motivated and not become disappointed by just barely missing your goal. This method also allows you to take advantage of continuous improvement.

Measure of Success for goal:

_____

_____

_____

Exercise 3: List the major tasks needed to achieve the goal. Don't allow yourself to become too weighed down in detail. One way to do this is by working backwards from the achievement of your goal to the first step needed to accomplish the goal. This is a great way to break large goals down into manageable chunks.

Tasks Necessary to Accomplish Goal:

_____

_____

_____

_____

_____

Exercise Four: Prioritizing
Make a point to spend some time assigning priority

ratings to the tasks that need to be accomplished in order to achieve your overall goal. Determine how much time is needed to complete each task and then prioritize the tasks so you always know what you need to be working on in order to attain this goal.

Weekly Plan

Date:

Activities Required to Accomplish Objectives	Priority	Time Needed	Day

Exercise 5: Timing

The process of assigning real dates as deadlines for completing activities has a strange way of increasing your success rate. If you do not already have one, make it a point to pick up a calendar or datebook and assign timelines to your tasks according to realistic expectations.

Exercise 6: Assess your desire for this goal

When considering the possibility of taking on a new goal it is extremely important you evaluate the level of your desire to accomplish the goal. Along the same regard you also must spend some time in determining whether you have the resources necessary to accomplish the goal.

Ability (skill)

Have I been taught to do this?

Do I see this as my role?

Do I know how to do this?

Have I successfully done this, or something similar, before?

Enthusiasm (will)

Do I want to do this? Does it correspond with my personal values?

What is the risk of failure? Am I comfortable with that risk of failure?

Do I believe I can do it?

Exercise 7: Evaluate your Goals

Always use the SMART model in order to evaluate your goals as well as take the time to determine what could have been done differently next time to make the achievement of your goal even more successful.

Evaluating Goals

Part of the process of evaluating your goals begins when you actually begin to form them. Remember each goal you set should meet the SMART system.

Specific

Measurable

Action-Oriented

Realistic

Time and Resource Constrained

Specific

All goals should be straightforward and specific. They should emphasize what it is that you want to happen and clearly define what it is you are going to do to accomplish that goal. Remember to concentrate on the following when creating specific goals:

What?
Why?
How?

WHAT are you going to do? Focus on using action words such as direct, organize, coordinate, lead, develop, plan, build, etc.

WHY is this goal important to accomplish at this time? What do you want to ultimately accomplish?

HOW are you going to do it? (By...)

Measurable

Remember if you can't measure a goal then you won't be able to manage it. Because of the fact you will frequently need to divide your goals up into smaller segments, this portion of the SMART model is even more important. You need to be able to measure even the small term goals in order to accomplish the overall larger goal.

Ask yourself how you will see it when the goal is reached. Take the time to establish concrete criteria for measuring progress toward the attainment of the goal. This will allow you to stay on track and reach your target dates.

Attainable

When you set goals that are out of your reach, it is quite likely that you will either be disappointed when you are not able to reach them or you won't even commit to trying to reach them at all. You will be able to give the process of obtaining your goals your best when you know that the goal is within your reach, even if it is challenging.

Realistic

Setting a realistic goal is not the same as setting an easy goal. Remember that in order for a goal to be realistic you must have the time and resources available in order to accomplish the goal. Obtaining the necessary resources may be one of the obstacles you will need to overcome in order to accomplish the goal, but you should be able to realistically do this. Be balanced in setting realistic goals. Remember that goals that are too difficult allow you to set yourself up for failure while goals that are too easy provide only a limited amount of accomplishment.

Timely

Always make it a point to set timeframes for your goals, whether this is in terms of days, weeks, months or even years. Put a specific ending point on it so that you have a target to work towards.

When evaluating your goals, it is also important to take a look at what has worked in the process and what could be improved upon in order to aid future goal projects. Consider these questions as evaluation tools:

1. What supports/resources worked best to help me achieve my goal(s)?
2. What problems did I encounter and how did I overcome them?
3. What progress did I make?
4. Was the timeframe I set to attain my goal(s) too fast or too slow?
5. Which objectives are still unmet?
6. What experiences did I find rewarding?
7. Which experiences were unrewarding?
8. Is the program working for me? Why or why not?
9. What recommendations can I make?

	Goal	How I did	The best thing about trying to reach this goal
1st			
2nd			
3rd			

Conclusion: The Importance of Belief in Accomplishing Goals

It is quite common for most of us to have a voice inside our heads that constantly nags at us and tells us that we cannot accomplish sometime. In some people that voice is stronger than others but if we are all honest and admit the truth, we will admit that it is there.

That voice can be detrimental to the process of goal setting. The success rate of our goals depends upon how we respond to that voice. Believing in your own ability to accomplish what may seem to be the impossible is the key element to succeeding in your goals. Event that negative voice inside your head can be changed by your own belief in yourself and your abilities. It is your positive outlook that will increase your self esteem as you remain focused on your goals and begin to seem them attained one by one.

Remember to never give up, always remain persistent and focused and above all; to believe in your ability to attain your dreams.

www.ingramcontent.com/pod-product-compliance
Lightning Source LLC
Chambersburg PA
CBHW071253170526
45165CB00003B/1323